Ancient Manners
Also Known As Aphrodite
(Book-II)

Pierre Louÿs

Alpha Editions

This Edition Published in 2021

ISBN: 9789355349842

Design and Setting By
Alpha Editions
www.alphaedis.com
Email – info@alphaedis.com

TABLE OF CONTENTS

BOOK II

I
THE GARDENS OF THE GODDESS

The temple of Aphrodite-Astarte stood outside the gates of the town, in an immense park, full of flowers and shade. The Nile water, conveyed by seven aqueducts, induced an extraordinary verdure all the year round.

This flowering forest on the sea's verge, these deep streams, these lakes, these darkling meadows, had been created in the desert more than two centuries previously by the first of the Ptolemies. Since then, the sycamores planted by his orders had grown to gigantic size; under the influence of the fertilising waters, the lawns had grown into meads, the basins had widened into ponds, nature had turned a park into a champaign.

The gardens were more than a valley, more than a country; they were a complete world enclosed by bounds of stone and governed by a goddess, the soul and centre of this universe. All around it stood a circular terrace, eighty stades long and thirty-two feet high. This was not a wall, it was a colossal "cité," composed of fourteen hundred houses. A corresponding number of prostitutes inhabited this sacred town, and in this unique spot were represented seventy different nationalities.

The plan of the sacred houses was uniform and as follows: the door, of red copper (a metal consecrated to the goddess), bore a phallos-shaped knocker which fell upon a receiving-plate in relief, the image of the cteis; and beneath was graved the courtesan's name, with the initials of the usual formula:

Ω.Ξ.Ε.
ΚΟΧΛΙΣ
Π.Π.Π

Two rooms contrived like shops opened out on either side of the door, that is to say, there was no wall on the side facing the gardens.

The one on the right, the "chambre exposée," was the place where the courtesan sat bedecked with her adornments upon a lofty cathedra at the hour when the men arrived. The one on the left was at the disposal of suitors who wished to pass the night in the open air, without, however, sleeping on the grass.

When the door was opened, a corridor gave access to a vast court-yard paved with marble, the centre of which was occupied by an oval basin. A peristyle cast a circle of shadow round this patch of light, and interposed a zone of coolness between it and the entries to the seven chambers of the house. At the further end rose the altar of red granite.

Each woman had brought a little idol of the goddess from her native country, and each adored it in her own tongue, as it stood upon the altar, without understanding the other women. Lachmi, Ashtaroth, Venus, Ischtar, Freia, Mylitta, Cypris, such were the religious names of their deified VOLUPTAS. Some venerated her under a symbolic form: a red pebble, a conical stone, a great knotted shell. Most of them had a little statuette on a pedestal of green wood, usually a rudely-carved figure with thin arms, heavy breasts, and excessive hips. The hand pointed to the delta-shaped locks of the belly. They laid a myrtle-branch at its feet, scattered the altar with rose leaves, and burned a little grain of incense for every prayer granted. It was the confidant of all their troubles, the witness of all their undertakings, the supposed cause of all their pleasures. At their death, it was placed in their fragile little coffin, to watch over their sepulture.

The most beautiful of these women came from the kingdoms of Asia. Every year, the vessels which carried the presents of the tributaries or allies to Alexandria landed, together with the bales and leathern bottles, a cargo of a hundred virgins chosen by the priests for the service of the sacred garden. They were Mysians and Jewesses, Phrygians and Cretans, daughters of Ecbatana and Babylon, maidens from the Bay of Pearls and from the sacred banks of the Ganges. Some were white-skinned with medallion-like faces and inflexible bosoms; others, brown as the earth under rain, wore silver rings in their noses. Their hair fell short and dark upon their shoulders.

Some came from a still greater distance: dainty, deliberate little beings, whose language nobody understood, and who resembled yellow monkeys.

Their long eyes pointed towards their temples; they dressed their straight black hair in the quaintest fashion. These girls remained all their lives as timid as strayed animals. They knew the movements of love, but refused the kiss upon the mouth. Between two passing unions they were to be seen sitting on their little feet, and playing with one another, and amusing themselves like infants.

In a solitary meadow, the pink and pale daughters of the North lived together, lying upon the grass. They were Sarmatians with triple tresses, robust legs, square shoulders, who made garlands for themselves with the branches of trees, and wrestled for a pastime. There were big-breasted, flat-nosed, hairy Scythians, who paired in the attitude of beasts; gigantic Teutons who terrified the Egyptians with their hair pale as that of old men and their flesh softer than that of children; Gauls, sandy-hued like cows, and who laughed without a motive; young Celts with sea-green eyes, who never went out naked.

Elsewhere, the brown-breasted Iberians assembled together during the day. They had heavy hair that they dressed with extreme care, and nervous bellies which they did not depilate. Their firm skins and powerful croups were held in great esteem by the Alexandrians. They were chosen for dancing-girls as often as for mistresses. Under the large shadow of the palm-trees lived the daughters of Africa: Numidians veiled in white, Carthaginians apparelled in black gauze, Negresses enveloped in many-coloured costumes.

They were fourteen hundred.

When once a woman had entered the garden, she never left it till the first day of her old age. She gave the half of her gains to the temple, and the remainder went to defray the cost of her meals and perfumes.

The poorer tradesman . . . preferred to address themselves to the women who slept thus in the open air.

They were not slaves, and each was the real owner of one of the houses of the Terrace; but all were not equally beloved, and the most fortunate often found the opportunity of buying the neighbouring houses, which their owners were willing to sell in order to escape the ravages of hunger. These girls carried off their obscene statuettes to the park and searched out a flat stone to serve as an altar, in a corner which henceforth they did not leave. The poorer tradesmen were aware of this. and preferred to address themselves to the women who slept thus in the open air upon the moss near their sanctuaries; but occasionally even these suitors were not forthcoming, and then the poor creatures took to themselves a partner in distress. These passionate friendships developed almost into conjugal love. The couple shared everything down to the last scrap of wool. They consoled one another for their long periods of chastity by alternate complaisances.

Those who had no girl friends offered themselves of their own accord as slaves to their more prosperous colleagues.

The latter were forbidden to have more than a dozen of these poor creatures in their service; but twenty-two courtesans were quoted as having attained the maximum. These had chosen a motley staff of domestics from all the nationalities.

If, in the course of their stray amours, they conceived a son, he was brought up in the temple-enclosure in the contemplation of the perfect form and in the service of its divinity. If they were brought to bed of a daughter, the child was consecrated to the goddess.

On the first day of its life, they celebrated its symbolic marriage with the son of Dionysos, and the Hierophant deflowered it herself with a little golden knife; for virginity is displeasing to Aphrodite. Later on, the little girl entered the Didascalion, a great monumental school situated behind the temple, and where the theory and practice of all the erotic arts were taught in seven stages: the use of the eyes, the embrace, the motions of the body, the secrets of the bite, of the kiss, and of glottism.

The pupil chose the day of her first experiment at her own good pleasure, because desire is ordained by the goddess, whose will must be obeyed. On that day, she was allotted one of the houses of the Terrace, and some of these children, who were not even nubile, counted amongst the most zealous and the most esteemed.

The interior of the Didascalion, the seven class-rooms, the little theatre, and the peristyle of the court, were decorated with ninety-two frescoes designed to sum up the whole of amatory teaching. It was the life-work of one man. Cleochares of Alexandria, the natural son and disciple of Apelles, had terminated them on the eve of his death. Recently, Queen Berenice, who was greatly interested in the celebrated school and sent her young sisters to it, had ordered a series of marble groups from Demetrios in order to complete the decoration; but as yet only one of them had been erected, in the children's class-room.

At the end of each year, in the presence of the entire body of courtesans, a great competition took place, which excited an extraordinary emulation amongst this crowd of women, for the twelve prizes which were offered conferred the right to the most exalted glory it was possible to dream of: the right to enter the Cotytteion.

This last monument was shrouded in so much mystery, that it is impossible for us to give a detailed description of it. We know merely that it was comprised in the peribola and that it had the form of a triangle of which the base was a temple of the goddess Cotytto, in whose name fearful unknown debauches took place. The other two sides of the monument were composed of eighteen houses; they were inhabited by thirty-six courtesans, so sought after by rich lovers that they did not give themselves for less than two minæ: they were the Baptes of Alexandria. Once a month, at full moon, they assembled in the temple enclosure, maddened by aphrodisiacs, and girt with the canonical phallos. The oldest of the thirty-six was required to take a mortal dose of the terrible erotogenous philter. The certainty of a speedy death impelled her to attempt without hesitation all the dangerous feats of sensual passion before which the living recoil. Her body, covered with foam, became the centre and model of the whirling orgie; in the midst of prolonged shriekings, cries, tears, and dances, the other naked women embraced her with frenzy, bathed their hair in her sweat, fastened on her burning flesh, and drew fresh ardors from the uninterrupted spasm of this furious agony. Three years these women lived thus, and such was the wild madness of their end at the close of the thirty-sixth month.

Other less venerated sanctuaries had been erected by the women, in honour of the other names of the multiform Aphrodite. There was an altar sacred to the Ouranian Aphrodite, which received the chaste vows of sentimental courtesans: another to the Apostrophian Aphrodite, who granted forgetfulness of unrequited loves; another to the Chrysean Aphrodite, who attracted rich lovers; another to Genetyllis, the patron goddess of women in child-birth; another to Aphrodite of Colias, who presided over gross passions, for everything which related to love fell within the pious cult of the goddess. But these special altars possessed no efficacy or virtue except in the case of unimportant desires. Their service was haphazard, their favours were a matter of daily occurrence, and their votaries were on terms of familiarity with them. Suppliants whose prayers had been granted made simple offerings of flowers; those who were not content defiled them with their excrements. They were neither consecrated nor kept up by the priests, and their profanation incurred no punishment.

Far different was the discipline of the temple.

The temple, the Great Temple of the Great Goddess, the most sacred spot in all Egypt, the inviolable Astarteïon, was a colossal edifice one hundred and thirty six feet in length, standing on the summit of the gardens and approached on all sides by seventeen steps. The golden gates were guarded by twelve hermaphrodite hierodules, symbolising the two objects of love and the twelve hours of the night.

The entrance did not face towards the east, but in the direction of Paphos, that is to say, towards the north-east. The sun's rays never penetrated directly into the sanctuary of the Great Goddess of the Night. Eighty-six columns upheld the architrave: they were tinted purple as far as their mid-height, and all the upper part stood out from these gaudy trappings with an unspeakable whiteness, like the busts of standing women.

Between the epistyle and the coronis, the long belt-shaped Zophora unfolded its bestial sculptures, erotic and fabulous. There were centauresses mounted by stallions, goats tumbled by meagre satyrs, virgins served by monstrous bulls, naïads covered by stags, bacchantes loved by tigers, lionesses seized by griffins. All this great wallowing multitude of beings was exalted by the irresistible divine passion. The male strained, the female opened, and the fusion of the creative forces produced the first thrill of life. The crowd of obscure couples sometimes, by chance, left a clear space round some immortal scene: Europa on hands and knees bearing the weight of the glorious Olympian beast; Leda guiding the hardy swan between her beautiful arched thighs. Farther on, the insatiable Siren exhausting expiring Glaucos; the god Pan standing upright and possessing an hamadryad with flying hair; the Sphinx raising her croup to the level of the horse Pegasos. At the end of the frieze, the sculptor had carved a figure of himself facing the goddess Aphrodite. He stood there modelling the contours of a perfect cteis in soft wax, with the goddess herself as his model, as if his whole ideal of beauty, joy, and virtue had long since taken refuge in this precious fragile flower.

II
MELITTA

"Purify thyself, stranger."

"I shall enter pure," said Demetrios.

Dipping the end of her hair in water, the young gate-keeper moistened first his eyelids, then his lips and fingers, in order that his glance might be sanctified, as also the kiss of his mouth and the caress of his hands.

And then he pressed forward into the wood of Aphrodite.

Through the dark branches, he perceived a setting sun of sombre purple, powerless to dazzle the eyes. It was the evening of the day on which his life had been convulsed by the meeting with Chrysis.

The feminine soul is of a simplicity incredible to men. Where there is nothing but a straight line, they obstinately search for the complexity of a web; they find emptiness and go astray in it. Thus it was that the soul of Chrysis, limpid as a little child's, appeared to Demetrios more mysterious than a problem in metaphysics. After leaving this woman upon the quay, he went back to his house like a man in a dream, incapable of answering all the questions which tormented him. What did she want with these three gifts? It was impossible for her either to wear or to sell a celebrated mirror, acquired by theft, the comb of an assassinated woman, the pearl necklace of the goddess. If she kept them at home, she would expose herself every day to the possibility of a fatal discovery. Then why ask for them? To destroy them? He knew only too well that women are incapable of enjoying things in secret and that good fortune brings them happiness only as soon as it is noised abroad. And then, what divination, what profound clairvoyance had led her to judge him capable of accomplishing three such extraordinary actions for her sake?

Assuredly, if he had liked, he might have carried off Chrysis from her home, held her at his mercy, and made her his mistress, his wife, or his slave, at choice. He had even the right to do away with her, simply. Former revolutions had accustomed the citizens to violent deaths, and no one would have troubled about the disappearance of a courtesan. Chrysis must know this, and yet she had dared . . .

The young gate-keeper moistened first his eyelids.

The more he thought about her, the more grateful he was to her for having varied the usual routine of bargaining in so charming a manner. How many women of equal worth with Chrysis had offered themselves clumsily! But what did this one ask for? Neither love, nor gold, nor jewels, but three unheard-of crimes! She interested him keenly. He had offered her all the treasures of Egypt: he felt distinctly, now, that if she had accepted them she would not have received two obols, and that he would have tired of her even before knowing her. Three crimes were certainly an unusual salary; but she was worthy to receive it since she was a woman capable of exacting it, and he promised himself to go on with the adventure.

In order not to give himself the time to repent of his firm resolve, he went the very same day to the house of Bacchis, found the house empty, took the silver mirror and went off to the gardens.

Was it necessary to make a direct call on Chrysis's second victim? Demetrios thought not. The priestess Touni, who owned the famous ivory comb, was so charming and so weak that he was afraid of repenting if he went straight to her house without any preliminary precautions. He retraced his steps and went along the Grand Terrace.

The courtesans were on show in their "chambres exposées" like flowers in a shop window.

Their attitudes and their costumes had no less diversity than their ages, types, and races. The most beautiful, according to the tradition of Phryne, leaving exposed nothing but the oval of their faces, sat enveloped from head to foot in their great garment of fine wool. Others had adopted the fashion of transparent robes, under which one distinguished their beauties mysteriously, just as, through limpid water, one discerns the green mosses lying in splashes of shade upon the bottom. Those whose sole charm consisted in their youthfulness sat naked to the waist, stiffening out their busts in order to display to the best advantage the firmness of their breasts. But the most mature, knowing that the features of the feminine visage age more quickly than the skin of the body, sat quite naked, holding their breasts in their hands, and stretching their clumsy thighs apart, as if they wished to prove that they were still women.

Demetrios passed slowly before them.

Demetrios passed slowly before them, with unflagging admiration. He had never yet succeeded in contemplating a woman's nudity without intense emotion. He understood neither disgust before the corpse of a young woman nor insensibility to the body of a little girl. That evening any woman could have charmed him. Provided she remained silent and did not display more ardour than the minimum required by the etiquette of the bed, he was quite ready to forgive her for her lack of beauty. And what is more, he even preferred that she should have a coarse body, for the more his intelligence considered faultless forms, the less room was there for his sensual desires. The agitation which he felt upon contact with living beauty was due to a sensualism exclusively cerebral, which annihilated mere sexual excitation. He remembered with anguish having remained all night as impotent as an old man, by the side of the most admirable woman he had ever held in his arms. And since that night he had learnt to choose mistresses of less purity.

"Friend," said a voice, "you don't recognise me?"

He turned round with a negative sign, and went on his way, for he never undressed the same woman twice. It was the principle that guided his visits to the gardens. A woman one has not yet possessed retains something of the virgin; but what good result, what surprise can one expect from a second rendez-vous? It is almost marriage. Demetrios did not expose himself to the illusions of the second night. Queen Berenice sufficed for his rare conjugal impulses, and with that exception he was careful to choose a new accomplice for every evening's indispensable adultery.

"Clonarion!

Gnatene!

Plango!

Mnaïs!

Crobyle!

Ioessa."

They cried their names as he passed, and some added protestations of their ardent natures or proposed an abnormal vice. Demetrios followed the road. He was preparing to choose at a venture, according to his habit, when a little girl entirely dressed in blue leaned her head upon her shoulder and said to him softly, without rising:

"Is it quite out of the question?"

The novelty of this mode of address made him smile. He stopped.

"Open the door," he said. "I choose you."

The little girl gleefully jumped to her feet and gave two raps with the phallus-shaped knocker. The door was opened by an old slave woman.

"Gorgo," said the little girl, "I have got somebody; quickly, get some cakes and Cretan wine, and make the bed."

She turned round to Demetrios.

"You don't want any satyrion?"

"No," said the young man laughing. "You have some?"

"I have to keep it," said the child. "I am asked for it oftener than you think. Come this way; be careful of the steps, one of them is worn. Go into my room. I shall be back in a moment."

The room was quite simple, like those of the novices. A great bed, a couch, a few seats and carpets composed all the scanty furniture; but through a large open bay there was a view over the gardens, the sea, the double harbour of Alexandria. Demetrios remained standing and looked at the distant city.

Suns setting behind harbours! Incomparable glories of maritime cities, calm skies, purple waters! Upon what soul vociferous with joy or sorrow would you not cast a shroud of silence? What feet have not halted, what passions have not withered, what voices have not died away before you? . . . Demetrios looked; a swell of torrential flame seemed to issue from the sun, half dipping into the sea, and to flow straight to the left bend of the wood of Aphrodite. From horizon to horizon, the Mediterranean was flooded by the sumptuous purple spectrum which lay in sharply-defined bands of colour, golden red and dull violet side by side. Between this ever-shifting splendour and the peaty mirror of Lake Mareotis, stood the white mass of the town, bathed in red and violet reflexions. Its twenty thousand flat houses spreading in different directions picked it out marvellously with twenty thousand dashes of colour that underwent a perpetual metamorphosis according to the various phases of the setting luminary. The flaming sun shot forth rapid shafts, then was swallowed up, almost suddenly, in the sea, and with the first reflux of the night, there floated over the whole earth a thrill, a muffled breeze, uniform and transparent.

"Here are figs, cakes, a piece of honeycomb, wine, a woman. Eat the figs while it is daylight and the woman when it is dark."

It was the little girl, laughing as she entered. She bade the young man sit down, mounted astride on his knees, and stretching her two arms behind her head, made fast a rose which was on the point of slipping down from her auburn hair.

In spite of himself Demetrios could not restrain an exclamation of surprise. She was completely naked, and when divested of her ample robe, her little body was seen to be so young, so infantine in the breast, so narrow at the hips, so visibly immature, that Demetrios felt a sense of pity, like a horseman on the point of throwing his man's weight upon an over-delicate mare.

"But you are not a woman!" he exclaimed.

"I am not a woman! By the two goddesses, what am I, then? A Thracian, a porter, or an old philosopher?"

"How old are you?"

"Ten and a half. Eleven. One may say eleven. I was born in the gardens. My mother is a Milesian. She is called Pythias, but she goes by the name of 'The Goat.' Shall I send for her, if you think me too little? Her house is not far from mine."

"You have been to the Didascalion?"

"I am still there in the sixth class. I shall have finished next year; and not too soon either."

"Aren't you happy?"

"Ah! if only you knew how difficult the mistresses are to please! They make you recommence the same lesson twenty times! Things perfectly useless that men never ask for. And then one is tired out, all for nothing. I don't like that at all. Come, take a fig; not that one, it is not ripe. I will show you a new way to eat. Look!"

"I know it. It is longer and no better than the other way. I see that you are a good pupil."

"Oh! I have learnt everything I know by myself. The mistresses would have us believe that they are cleverer than we are. They have more style, that may be, but they have invented nothing."

"You have many lovers?"

"They are all too old: it is inevitable. Young men are so foolish! They only like women forty years old. Now and again I see young men pretty as Eros pass by, and if you were to see what they choose! Hippopotami! It is enough to make one turn pale. I hope sincerely that I shall never reach these women's age: I should be too ashamed to undress. I am so glad to be still quite young. The breasts always develop too soon. I think that the first month I see my blood flow I shall feel ready to die. Let me give you a kiss. I like you very much."

Here the conversation took a less serious if not a more silent turn, and Demetrios rapidly perceived that his scruples were beside the mark in the case of so expert a young lady. She seemed to realise that she was somewhat meagre pasturage for a young man's appetite, and she battled her lover by a prodigious activity of furtive finger-touches, which he could neither foresee nor elude, nor direct, and which never left him the leisure for a loving embrace. She multiplied her agile, firm little body around him, offered herself, refused herself, slipped and turned and struggled. Finally they grasped one another. But this half hour was merely a long game.

She jumped out of bed the first, dipped her finger in the honey-bowl and moistened her lips; then, making a thousand efforts not to laugh, she bent over Demetrios and rubbed her mouth against his. Her round curls danced on either side of their cheeks. The young man smiled and leaned upon his elbow.

"What is your name?" he asked.

"Melitta. Did you not see my name upon the door?"

"I did not look."

"You can see it in my room. They have written it all over the walls. I shall soon be forced to have them repainted."

Demetrios raised his head: the four panels of the chamber were covered with inscriptions.

"That is very curious, indeed." said he. "May one read?"

"Oh, if you like. I have no secrets."

He read. Melitta's name was there several times repeated, coupled with various men's names and barbaric drawings. Tender, obscene, or comic sentences jostled oddly with one another. Lovers boasted of their vigour, or detailed the charms of the little courtesan, or poked fun at her girl-friends. All this was interesting merely as a written proof of a general degradation. But, looking towards the bottom of the right-hand panel, Demetrios gave a start.

"What is that? What is that? Speak!"

"Who? What? Where?" said the child. "What is the matter with you?"

"Here. That name. Who wrote that?"

And his finger stopped under this double line.

ΜΕΛΙΤΤΑ .Λ. ΧΡΥΣΙΔΑ
ΧΡΥΣΙΣ .Λ. ΜΕΛΙΤΤΑΝ

"Ah!" she answered, "that's me. I wrote that."

"Who is she, Chrysis?"

"My great friend."

"I dare say. That is not what I ask you. Which Chrysis? There are many."

"Mine, the most beautiful. Chrysis of Galilee."

"You know her! you know her! But speak, speak! Where does she come from? where does she live? who is her lover? tell me everything!"

He sat down upon the couch and took the little girl upon his knees.

"You are in love, then?" she said.

"That matters little to you. Tell me what you know; I am in a hurry to hear everything."

"Oh! I know nothing at all. It is quite short. She has been to see me twice, and you may imagine that I have not asked her for details about her family. I was too happy to have her, and I did not lose time in conversation."

"How is she made?"

"Like a pretty girl, what do you expect me to say? Do you want me to name all the parts of her body, adding that everything is beautiful? And then, she is a woman, a real woman . . . Every time I think about her I desire somebody."

And she put her arm round the neck of Demetrios.

"Don't you know anything about her?" he began again.

"I know—I know that she comes from Galilee, that she is nearly twenty years old, and that she lives in the Jews' quarter, in the east end, near the gardens. But that is all."

"And about her life, her tastes? can you tell me nothing? She is fond of women, since she came to see you. But is she altogether Lesbian?"

"Certainly not. The first night she passed here, she brought a lover, and I swear to you there was no make-believe about her. When a woman is sincere, I can see it by her eyes. That did not prevent her from returning once quite alone. And she has promised me a third night."

"You don't know whether she has any other *amie* in the gardens? Nobody?"

"Yes, one of her countrywomen, Chimairis. She is very poor."

"Where does she live? I must see her."

"She has slept in the wood for upwards of a year. She has sold her house. But I know where her den is. I can take you to it if you wish. Put on my sandals, will you?"

Demetrios rapidly buckled the plaited leather straps round Melitta's slender ankles. Then he handed her her short robe, which she merely threw over her arm, and they departed in haste.

—

They walked far. The park was immense. From time to time, a girl under a tree proffered her name and opened her robe, then lay down again and leaned her face upon her hand. Melitta knew some of them: they embraced her without stopping her. Passing before a rustic altar, she gathered three great flowers and placed them upon the stone.

"My little girl! my little love! how are you?"

It was not yet dusk. The intense light of summer days has something permanent about it which lingers vaguely in the slow twilight.

The faint, humid stars, hardly brighter than the body of the sky, twinkled and throbbed gently, and the shadows of the branches remained indecisive.

"Mamma! There's mamma," cried Melitta suddenly.

A woman, dressed in a garment of triple muslin striped with blue, was seen advancing with a tranquil step, alone. As soon as she caught sight of the child she ran up to her, raised her off the ground, lifted her up in her arms, and kissed her energetically on the cheek.

"My little girl! my little love! how are you?"

"I am guiding somebody who wants to see Chimairis. And you? Are you out for a walk?"

"Corinna is *accouchée*. I have been to see her. I have dined by her bedside."

"And what has she given birth to? A boy?"

"Two twin girls, my dear, as pink as wax dolls. You can go and see them tonight; she will show them to you."

"Oh! how lovely! Two little courtesans. What are their names?"

"They are both called Pannychis, because they were born on the day before the Aphrodisiæ. It is a divine presage. They will be pretty."

She replaced the child upon her feet, and turning to Demetrios:

"What do you think of my daughter? Have I the right to be proud of her?"

"You have the right to be satisfied with one another," he answered gravely.

"Kiss mamma," said Melitta.

He silently imprinted a kiss between her breasts. Pythias returned it to him upon the mouth, and they separated.

Demetrios and the child advanced a few more paces beneath the trees, whilst the courtesan receded into the distance, turning her head as she walked. At last they reached their goal, and Melitta said:

"It is here."

Chimairis was sitting crouching upon her left heel, on a little grass-plot between two trees and a bust. A sort of red rag, her last remaining day garment, lay spread out beneath her. At night, she slept upon it naked, at the hour the men passed. Demetrios contemplated her with growing interest. She had the feverish aspect of certain emaciated dark women whose tawny bodies seem consumed by an ever-throbbing ardour. Her powerful lips, the excessive brilliancy of her glance, her livid eyelids combined to produce a double expression of sensual lustfulness and physical exhaustion. The curve of her hollow belly and her nervous thighs formed a natural cavity, designed as if to receive; and as she had sold everything, even her combs and pins, even her depilatory tweezers, her hair was tangled together in inextricable disorder. A black pubescence invested her nudity with a certain savage and shaggy effrontery.

A great he-goat stood stiffly on its four legs beside her. It was tethered to a tree by a gold chain which had formerly glittered in a quadruple coil upon its mistress's breast.

"Chimairis," said Melitta, "get up. Here is somebody who wishes to speak to you."

The Jewess looked, but did not move.

Demetrios advanced.

"Do you know Chrysis?" he said.

"Yes."

"Do you see her often?"

"Yes."

"Will you talk to me about her?"

"No."

"What? No? What? you cannot?"

"No."

Melitta was stupefied.

"Speak to him," she said. "Have confidence. He loves her, he wishes her well."

"I see clearly that he loves her." answered Chimairis. "If he loves her, he wishes her ill. If he loves her, I shall not speak."

Demetrios tingled with rage, but said nothing.

"Give me your hand," said the Jewess. "It will tell me whether I am mistaken."

She took the young man's left hand and turned it towards the moonlight. Melitta leaned forward to see, although she could not read the mysterious lines, but their fatality attracted her.

"What do you see?" said Demetrios.

"I see . . . Can I tell what I see? will you be obliged to me? First I see happiness, but it is all in the past. I also see love, but it is drowned in blood . . ."

"In my blood?"

"In a woman's blood. And then the blood of another woman. And then yours, a little later on."

Demetrios shrugged his shoulders, and when he turned, he perceived Melitta fleeing down the alley at full speed.

"It has given her a fright," said Chimairis.

"But there is no question of Melitta or of me. Let things take their course, since nothing can be prevented. Your destiny was certain even before your birth. Go. I shall say no more." And she dropped his hand.

III
LOVE AND DEATH

"A woman's blood. Afterwards another woman's blood. Afterwards yours, but a little later on."

Demetrios repeated these words to himself as he walked, and in spite of himself, his belief in them weighed upon him. He had never had any faith in oracles drawn from the bodies of victims or the movements of planets. These affinities seemed too problematical. But the complex lines of the hand have, in themselves, an exclusively personal horoscopic aspect which he considered with uneasiness. The fortune-teller's prediction haunted his mind.

In his turn, he examined the palm of his left hand, on which his life was summed up in secret and indelible signs.

In the first place he saw, at the summit, a sort of regular crescent, the ends of which pointed towards the base of the fingers. Below this, a deep quadruple line, knotted and roseale, marked in two places by very red spots. Another line, but thinner, ran parallel to this at first, and then swerved brusquely round towards the wrist. Finally, a third line, short and clear, turned round the base of the thumb, which was entirely covered with thread-like markings. He saw all that; but, not being able to read the hidden symbol, he passed his hand over his eyes and changed the subject of his meditations.

Chrysis! Chrysis! Chrysis! This name throbbed within him like a fever. Satisfy her, vanquish her, clasp her in his arms, fly with her elsewhere, to Syria, to Greece, to Rome, no matter where, provided it was a place where he had no mistress and she no lovers: that was the thing, and immediately, immediately.

Of the three presents she had asked for, one was already in his possession. Remained the other two: the comb and the necklace.

"The comb first," he said to himself.

Every evening at sunset, the high priest's wife went forth and sat upon a marble seat, with her back turned to the forest and her face set to the great expanse of sea in front of her. Demetrios knew this well, for this woman, like so many others, had been in love with him, and she had told him that the day he chose to possess her it was there he would find her.

It was to that spot, then, that he directed his steps. And there indeed she was; but she did not see him coming. She was sitting with her eyes shut, with her body thrown back upon the seat, and her arms hanging negligently by her sides.

She was an Egyptian. Her name was Touni. She wore a light tunic of bright purple, without clasp or girdle, and without other adornments than two black stars to mark the points of her breasts. The thin tissue, ironed into pleats, terminated at the curve of the delicate knees, and little shoes of blue leather, fitting like gloves, covered her dainty round feet. Her skin was very swarthy, her lips very thick, her shoulders very small, and her fragile, supple waist seemed to bend under the weight of her full throat. She was asleep with her mouth open, dreaming peacefully.

Demetrios, noiselessly, sat down on the bench, by her side.

He slowly drew nearer and nearer, leaning over her, appreciating the delicate lines of her smooth, dark-skinned shoulders, slender at the summit, muscular near the armpit and joined to the bust by the shading of the bush beneath.

Lower down, the long, loose slit of the purple muslin tunic was open as far as the hips. Through the gaping drapery, Demetrios slowly passed his hand, and his united finger-tips touched the curves of her left breast, damp with perspiration. Its nipple rose erect in the palm of his hand. Notwithstanding, Touni slept on.

Her dream gradually changed, but did not fade. Her breath came quicker through her half open lips and she murmured a long, unintelligible sentence, as her fevered head fell back once more.

With the same stealthy tenderness, Demetrios withdrew his hot hand, to let it be refreshed by the light breeze.

She was asleep.... dreaming peacefully.

From the vague outline of the blue garden slopes as far as the immense scintillation of the night, shuddered the eternal sea. Like unto another bosom of some fresh priestess, its undulations were swelling heavenwards, uplifted by the dreams of antiquity that still cause it to thrill in the sight of our belated glances. When the end of all things is nigh, the last living beings will try before they disappear to fathom the mysteries of the moving ocean.

The moon inclined her great goblet of blood over the waters. Far away, in the purest atmosphere that had ever united heaven and earth, a slight red trail, where black veins meandered, trembled on the surface of the waves beneath the rising orb of night, as when the agitation of a caress on a rounded breast, in the dead of night, remains long after the hand that caused it has been lifted.

Touni still slumbered, her head leaning backwards, her body well-nigh naked, enshrouded in tinted muslin folds.

The purple glare of the moon, as yet on the horizon, came over the sea towards the sleeping woman. The fatal, vivid rays lit her up with a flame that seemed immobile. Little by little, their brilliancy mounted, encircling the Egyptian girl. Her black curls appeared one by one, and finally the Comb flashed out of the darkness: the royal Comb that Chrysis coveted. The ivory diadem was now bathed in the glory of the crimson moonbeams.

It was then that the sculptor took Touni's sweet face in both his hands, turning her features towards his own. Her eyes opened and became dilated.

"Demetrios! Demetrios! Is it you? Oh! You have come at last! You are here!" she murmured, clasping him in her arms, as her voice rang with the accents of happiness. "Is it really you, Demetrios, whose hands awake me? Is it you, son of my goddess; God of my body and my life?"

Demetrios made as if to retreat. With one bound, she was close to him again.

"What do you fear?" she said. "For you I am not the woman before whom all tremble, because she is surrounded by the might of the High Priest. Forget my name, Demetrios. In their lovers' arms, women have no name. I am no longer what you think. I am nothing but a woman who loves and whose yearning for you fills her frame as far as the points of her breasts."

Demetrios did not open his lips.

"Listen to me a little while longer," she went on. "I know who enthrals you. I will not even be your mistress, nor make the least attempt to rival the queen. No, Demetrios. Do with me as you will. Take me like some little slave-wench that a man possesses for a few minutes, leaving her afterwards with a remembrance that becomes oblivion. Take me like the lowest poverty-stricken harlot who, crouching by the roadside, awaits the charity of some furtive and brutal attack of lust. After all, what am I to place myself above those women? Have the Immortals given me anything more than that with which they have endowed the most servile of all my slaves? You, at least, are Beauty incarnate, with its out spreading emanations of the Gods."

Demetrios, more steadfastly serious than before, pierced her with his glance.

"Wretched creature, what do you suppose emanates from the Gods, if it be not. — "

"Love!"

"Or Death!"

"What mean you?" she exclaimed, starting to her feet. "Death! Yes, Death indeed! But it is so far off for me! In sixty years' time, I'll think of my end. Why speak to me of Death, Demetrios?"

"Death this very night!" he said quietly.

She laughed outright, in sheer fright.

"Tonight? No, no! Who says so? Why should I die? Answer me! Speak! What means this vile mockery?"

"You are condemned."

"By whom?"

"By your destiny."

"How know you that?"

"Because my destiny is interwoven with yours, Touni."

"Is it my fate to die now?"

"It is your lot to die by my hand, on that bench."

He seized her wrist.

"Demetrios!" she stammered, affrighted. "I'll not shriek! I'll not call for aid! Only let me speak first!" She wiped the sweat from her brow. "If death—should come from you—death will be sweet—for me. I accept it; I desire it, but hearken!"

Staggering from stone to stone, she led him away in the dark night of the woods.

"Since in your hands are all the gifts of the Gods," she continued, "the first thrill of life and the final throb of agony, let both your palms, bestowing all they hold, be opened to my eyes, Demetrios. Give me the hand of Love as well as that of Death. If you do this, I die without regret."

There was no reply in the vague look he gave her, but she thought she read the "Yes" he had not uttered.

Transfigured a second time, she lifted towards him a new face, where desire, born again, drove, with the strength of desperation, all terror away.

"Demetrios!" she stammered, affrighted.

She spoke no more, but already between her lips that were never to close again, each breath she drew sang a soft song, as if she was beginning to feel the deepest voluptuousness of love before even being gripped in the conjunction she craved.

Nevertheless, she gained this supreme victory.

With one movement, she tore off her light tunic and rolled it up into a ball of muslin that she threw behind her, smiling with scarce a vestige of sadness. Her young and slender body was outstretched in such great and lively felicity that it was impossible for it not to be eternal, and as her preoccupied lover, who perhaps was merely anxiously hesitating, terminated the work of Love without beginning that of Death, she suddenly exclaimed:

"Ah! Kill me! Kill me, I say, Demetrios! Why do you tarry?"

He rose up a little, resting on his hands; looked once more at Touni, whose great eyes peered ecstatically in his face, from beneath him, and drawing out one of the long, golden hairpins that glittered behind her ears, he drove it deliberately home under her left breast.

IV
MOONLIGHT

Nevertheless, this woman would have given him her comb and her hair also, for love's sake.

If he did not ask for it, it was because he had scruples. Chrysis had very categorically demanded a crime, and not such or such old jewel stuck in a young woman's hair. That is why he considered it his duty to consent to bloodshed.

He might have reflected, too, that the vows one makes to women during the first heat of passion may be forgotten in the interval without any great detriment to the moral worth of the lover who has sworn them, and that if ever this involuntary forgetfulness deserved to be excused it was certainly in a case where the life of another woman, assuredly innocent, was also in the scales. But Demetrios did not trouble himself with this method of reasoning. The adventure upon which he was engaged seemed to him too curious to allow of his juggling away its violent incidents. He was afraid that, later on, he might regret having cut out of the plot a scene which, though short, was indispensable for the beauty of the *ensemble*. A feeble truckling to virtue is often all that is required to reduce a tragedy to the common-places of everyday existence. The death of Cassandra, he mused, is not absolutely necessary for the development of Agamemnon; but if it had not taken place, the whole Orestes Trilogy would have been spoilt.

And so, after cutting the storied comb out of Touni's hair, he stowed it away in his garments, and, without further reflection thereon, undertook the third of the labours ordained by Chrysis: the seizing of Aphrodite's necklace.

It was useless to dream of entering the temple by the main door. The twelve hermaphrodites who guarded the entrance would certainly have allowed Demetrios to pass, in spite of the order directing the exclusion of every profane person in the absence of the priests; but he had no need to prove his future guilt in this ingenuous manner, since a secret entrance led to the sanctuary.

Demetrios betook himself to a part of the wood which sheltered the Necropolis of the high priests of the goddess. He counted the first tombs, opened the door of the seventh, and closed it again behind him.

With great difficulty, for the stone was heavy, he raised the burial-slab under which a marble staircase plunged down into the earth, and he descended step by step.

He knew that sixty paces were to be made in a straight line, and that afterwards it would be necessary to feel one's way along the wall in order not to knock against the subterranean staircase of the temple.

The exceeding freshness of the deep earth calmed him little by little.

In a few minutes he arrived at the limit.

He mounted the stairs, and pushed open the trap-door.

—

The night was clear without, and pitch dark within the divine enclosure. When he had softly and carefully closed the resounding door, a chill fell upon him, and he felt as though hemmed in by the coldness of the stones. He dared not raise his eyes. This black silence terrified him: the darkness became alive with the unknown. He put his hand to his forehead like a man who does not want to awake for fear of finding himself among the living. At last he looked.

He saw, in a glory of moonbeams, the dazzling figure of the goddess. She stood upon a pedestal of pink stone laden with pendent treasures. She was naked and fully sexed, vaguely tinted with the natural colours of woman. With one hand, she held a mirror with a priapus handle, and with the other she adorned her beauty with a seven-stringed pearl necklace. One pearl larger than the others, long and silvery, shone between her two nipples like a nocturnal crescent between two rounded clouds. And they were the real sacred pearls born of the water-drops which had rolled into the shell of Anadyomene.

Demetrios lost himself in ineffable adoration.

Demetrios lost himself in ineffable adoration. He believed in very truth that Aphrodite herself was there. He did not recognise his handiwork, for the abyss between what he had been and what he had become was profound. He stretched out his arms and murmured the mysterious words of prayer which are used in the Phrygian ceremonies.

Supernatural, luminous, impalpable, naked, and pure, the vision floated upon the stone, palpitated gently. He fixed his eyes upon it, dreading lest the caress of his glance should cause this frail hallucination to dissolve into thin air. He advanced very softly, touched the pink heel with his finger, as if to make sure of the statue's existence, and, incapable of resisting the powerful attraction it exercised upon him, mounted to its side, laid his hands upon the white shoulders, and gazed into its eyes.

He trembled, he grew faint, he began to laugh with joy. His hands wandered over the naked arms, pressed the hard, cold bust, descended along the legs, caressed the globe of the belly. He hugged this immortality to his breast with all his might. He looked at himself in the mirror, he lifted up the pearl necklace, he took it off, he made it glitter in the moonlight, and put it back again, fearfully. He kissed the bended hand, the round neck, the wave-like throat, the parted marble lips. Then he stepped back to the edge of the pedestal, and, taking the divine arms in his hands, tenderly gazed at the adorable head.

The hair was dressed in the Oriental style, and veiled the forehead slightly. The half-closed eyes prolonged themselves in a smile. The lips were parted, as in the swoon of a kiss. He silently arranged the seven rows of pearls upon the glittering breast, and descended to the ground to contemplate the idol at a distance.

Then he became conscious of an awakening. He remembered what he had come to do, what he had wished to accomplish, what he had barely escaped accomplishing: a monstrous deed. He flushed to the temples.

The recollection of Chrysis passed before his memory like a vision of grossness. He enumerated all the flaws in her beauty: the thick lips, the heavy knees, the loose gait. He had forgotten what her hands were like; but he imagined them large, to add an odious detail to the image he abhorred. His mental state became similar to that of a man surprised at dawn by his mistress in the bed of an ignoble prostitute, and unable to explain to himself how he had allowed himself to be tempted the night before. He could find neither an excuse nor a serious reason. Evidently, throughout one day, he had been the victim of a sort of temporary madness, a physical perturbation, a disease. He felt that he was cured, though still drunk with giddiness.

In order to complete his recovery, he planted himself against the temple wall and remained standing for a long time before the statue. The light of the moon continued to descend through the square opening in the roof; Aphrodite was resplendent; and, as the eyes were veiled in shade, he sought to meet their glance.

The whole night passed thus. Then daylight came and the statue took on in succession the rosy lividness of the dawn and the gilded reflection of the sun.

Demetrios had ceased to think. The ivory comb and the silver mirror which he carried in his tunic had slipped from his memory. He abandoned himself voluptuously to serene contemplation.

Outside, a tempest of bird-songs twittered, whistled, sang in the garden. Women's voices were heard, talking and laughing at the foot of the walls. The bustle of the early morning arose from the awakened earth. Demetrios experienced nothing but feelings of bliss.

The sun was already high, and the shadow of the roof had already shifted when he heard a confused sound of light feet upon the outer flight of steps.

It was doubtless a sacrifice to be offered to the goddess, a procession of young women coming to carry out or utter vows before the statue, for the first day of the Aphrodisiæ.

Demetrios resolved to fly.

The sacred pedestal opened at the back, in a way known only to the priests and the sculptor. It was there that the hierophant stood to dictate to a young girl whose voice was clear and high the miraculous discourses which issued from the statue on the third day of the fête. Thence one might reach the gardens. Demetrios entered, and stopped before the bronze-plated openings which pierced the massive stone.

The two golden doors swung heavily open. Then the procession entered.

V
THE INVITATION

Towards the middle of the night, Chrysis was awakened by three knocks at the door.

She had slept all day between the two Ephesians, and, but for the disorder of their bed, they might have been taken for three sisters together. The Galilæan's thigh, bathed in perspiration, rested heavily upon Rhodis nestling up against her hostess. Myrtocleia was asleep upon her breast, with her face in her arm and her back uncovered.

A sound of voices was heard in the entrance.

Chrysis disengaged herself with great care, stepping over her companions, and getting down from the couch, held the door ajar.

"Who is it, Djala? Who is it?" she asked.

"It is Naukrates who wants to see you. I have told him you are not at liberty."

"What nonsense! Certainly I am at liberty! Enter, Naukrates, I am in my room."

And she went back to bed.

Naukrates remained for some time on the threshold, as if fearing to commit an indiscretion. The two music-girls opened their sleep-laden eyes and made efforts to tear themselves away from their dreams.

"Sit down," said Chrysis. "There is no need for coquetry between us. I know that you do not come for me. What do you want of me?"

Naukrates was a philosopher of repute, who had been Bacchis's lover for more than twenty years, and did not deceive her, more from indolence than fidelity. His grey hair was cut short, his beard pointed à la Demosthenes, and his moustache cropped so as not to hide his lips. He wore a large white garment made of simple wool with a plain stripe.

"I am the bearer of an invitation," he said. "Bacchis is giving a dinner to-morrow, to be followed by a fête. We shall be seven, with you. Don't fail to come."

"A fête? A propos of what?"

"She is to liberate her most beautiful slave, Aphrodisia. There will be dancing-girls and flute-girls. I think that your two friends are engaged to be there, and, as a matter of fact, they ought not to be here now. The rehearsal is going on at Bacchis's at this very moment."

"Oh! it is true," cried Rhodis, "we had forgotten about it. Get up, Myrto, we are very late."

But Chrysis protested.

"No, not yet! how disagreeable of you to steal away my women. If I had suspected that, I would not have let you in. Why, they are actually ready!"

"Our robes are not complicated," said the child. "And we are not beautiful enough to spend much time in dressing."

"I shall see you at the temple, of course?"

"Yes, to-morrow morning, we are going to offer doves. I am taking a drachma out of your purse, Chrysis, otherwise we should have nothing to buy them with. Good-bye till to-morrow."

They ran out. Naucrates considered for a short time the door that had just closed upon them; then he folded his arms and, turning round to Chrysis, said in a low voice:

"Good. Your behaviour is charming."

"What do you mean?"

"One woman is not enough for you. You must have two, now. You even pick them up in the street. It is a noble example you are setting. But kindly tell me what is to become of us men? You have all got little *amies*, and after quitting their insatiable arms, you have just as much passion to offer as they are willing to leave you. Do you think this can go on indefinitely? If things continue like this, we shall be forced to apply to Bathyllos . . ."

"Ah! no!" cried Chrysis. "You will never get me to admit that! I know well that people make the comparison, but it is entirely absurd; and I am astonished that you, who pretend to be a thinker, do not understand how ridiculous it is."

"And what difference do you see?"

"It is not a question of difference. There is no connection between the one and the other: that's clear!"

"I do not say you are wrong. I want to know your reasons."

"Oh! I can tell them you in two words: listen carefully. From the point of view of love, woman is a perfect instrument. From head to foot she is constructed, solely, marvellously, for love. *She alone knows how to love. She alone knows how to be loved.* Consequently, if a couple of lovers is composed of two women, it is perfect; if there is only one woman, it is only half as good; if there is no woman at all, it is purely idiotic. That is all I have to say."

"You are hard on Plato, my girl."

"Great men are not, any more than the gods, great under all circumstances. Pallas understands nothing about painting; Plato did not know how to love. Philosophers, poets, or rhetoricians, all who follow him, are as worthless as their master, and however admirable they may be in their art, in love they are devoid of knowledge. Believe me, Naukrates, I feel that I am right."

The philosopher made a gesture.

"I can tell Bacchis that she may count on you?" he said.

"You are somewhat wanting in reverence," he said; "but I do not by any means think you are wrong. My indignation was not real. There is something charming in the union of two young women, on condition that they both consent to remain feminine, keep their hair long, uncover their breasts, and refrain from arming themselves with adventitious instruments, as if they were illogically envious of the gross sex for which they profess such a pretty contempt. Yes, their liaison is remarkable because their caresses are entirely superficial, and the quality of their sensual satisfaction is all the more refined. They do not clasp one another in a violent embrace, they touch one another lightly in order to taste of the supreme joy. Their wedding-night is not defiled with blood. They are virgins, Chrysis. They are ignorant of the brutal action; this constitutes their superiority over Bathyllos, who maintains that he offers the equivalent, forgetting that you also, even in this sorry respect, could enter into competition with him. Human love is to be distinguished from the rut of animals only by two divine functions: the caress and the kiss. Now these are the only two functions known to the women in question. They have even brought them to perfection."

"Excellent," said Chrysis in astonishment. "But then what have you to reproach me with?"

"My grievance is that there are a hundred thousand of you. Already a great number of women only derive perfect pleasure from their own sex. Soon you will refuse to receive us altogether, even as a makeshift. It is from jealousy that I blame you."

At this point Naukrates considered that the conversation had lasted long enough, and he rose to his feet, simply.

"I can tell Bacchis that she may count on you?" he said.

"I will go," answered Chrysis.

The philosopher kissed her knees and slowly went out.

——

Then she joined her hands together and spoke aloud though she was alone.

"Bacchis . . . Bacchis . . . he comes from her house and he does not know! The mirror is still there, then! . . . Demetrios has forgotten me . . . If he has hesitated the first day, I am lost, he will do nothing. But is it possible that all is finished? Bacchis has other mirrors which she uses more often. Doubtless she does not know yet. Gods! Gods! no means of having news, and perhaps . . . Ah! Djala! Djala!"

The slave-woman entered.

"Give me my knuckle-bones," said Chrysis. "I want to tell my own fortune."

She tossed the four little bones into the air.

"Oh . . . Oh . . . Djala, look! the Aphrodite throw!"

This was the name given to a very rare throw whereby all the knuckle-bones presented a different face. The odds against this combination were exactly thirty-five to one. It was the best throw in the game.

Djala remarked coldly:

"What did you ask for?"

"It is true," said Chrysis, disappointed. "I forgot to wish. I certainly had something in my mind, but I said nothing. Does that count all the same?"

"I think not; you must begin again."

Chrysis cast the bones again.

"The Midas throw, this time. What do you think of that?"

"One cannot tell. Good or bad. It is a throw which is interpreted by the next one. Now start with a single bone."

Chrysis consulted the game a third time; but as soon as the bone fell, she stammered:

"The . . . the Chian ace!"

And she burst into sobs.

Djala too was uneasy, and said nothing. Chrysis wept upon the bed, with her hair lying in confusion about her head. At last she turned round angrily.

"Why did you make me begin again? I am sure the first throw counted."

"If you wished, yes. If not, no. You alone know," said Djala.

"Besides, the bones prove nothing. It is a Greek game. I don't believe in it. I shall try something else."

She dried her tears and crossed the room. She took a box of white counters from a shelf, counted out twenty-two, then with the point of a pearl clasp, engraved in succession the twenty-two letters of the Hebrew alphabet. They were the arcana of the Cabbala she had learnt in Galilee.

"I have confidence in this. This does not deceive", she said. "Lift up the skirt of your robe; I will use it as a bag."

She cast the twenty-two counters into the slave's tunic, repeating mentally:

"Shall I wear Aphrodite's necklace? Shall I wear Aphrodite's necklace? Shall I wear Aphrodite's necklace?"

And she drew the tenth arcanam, and this signified plainly:

"Yes."

An old white-bearded priest preceded the youthful band.

VI
CHRYSIS'S ROSE

It was a procession, white and blue and yellow and pink and green.

Thirty courtesans advanced, bearing baskets of flowers, snow-white doves with red feet, veils of the most fragile azure, and precious ornaments.

An old white-bearded priest, swathed to the head in stiff unbleached cloth, preceded the youthful band and guided the line of bending worshippers to the altar of stone.

They sang, and their song languished like the sea, sighed like a southern breeze, panted like an amorous mouth. The first two carried harps which they rested upon the hollow of their left hand and which curved forward like sickles of slender wood.

━━

One of them advanced and said:

"Tryphera, O beloved Cypris, offers thee this blue veil which she has woven herself, that thou mayest continue to deal gently with her."

━━

Another:

"Mousarion places at thy feet, O goddess of the beautiful coronal, these wreaths of wall-flowers and this bouquet of drooping daffodils. She has borne them in the orgie and has invoked thy name in the wild ecstasy of their perfumes, O! victorious one! have respect to these spoils of love."

━━

Yet another:

"As an offering to thee, golden Cytherea, Timo consecrates this spiral bracelet. Mayest thou entwine vengeance round the throat of her thou wottest of, even as this silver serpent entwined itself around her naked arms."

———

Myrtocleia and Rhodis advanced, holding one another by the hand.

"Here are two doves of Smyrna, with wings white as caresses, with feet red as kisses.

"O! double goddess of Amathontis, accept them of our joined hands, if it be true that the tender Adonis is not alone sufficient for thee and that sometimes thy sleep is retarded by a yet sweeter embrace."

———

A very young courtesan followed:

"Aphrodite Peribasia, receive my virginity with this blood-stained tunic. I am Pannychis of Pharos: I have dedicated myself to thee since last night."

———

Another:

"Dorothea conjures thee, O charitable Epistrophia to remove far from her spirit the desire that Eros has implanted in it, or else to inflame for her the eyes of him that says her nay. She offers thee this branch of myrtle, because it is the tree thou lovest best."

———

Another:

"On thine altar, O Paphia, Callistion places sixty silver drachmæ, the balance of four minæ she received from Cleomenos. Give her a lover still more generous if thou thinkest it a goodly offering."

———

There remained before the altar only a blushing little child who had occupied the last place in the procession. She held nothing in her hand but a little crocus wreath, and the priest scorned her for the poverty of her offering.

She said:

"I am not rich enough to give you silver coins, O glittering Olympian goddess. Besides, what could I give thee that thou lackest? Here are flowers, yellow and green, pleated into a wreath for thy feet. And now . . ."

She unbuckled the clasps of her tunic; the tissue slipped down to the ground and she stood revealed quite naked.

. . . "I dedicate myself to thee body and soul, beloved goddess. I desire to enter thy gardens and die a courtesan of the temple. I swear to desire naught but love, I swear to love but to love, I renounce the world and I shut myself up in thee."

—

Then the priest covered her with perfumes and enveloped her nudity in the veil woven by Tryphera. They left the nave together by the door opening into the gardens.

The procession seemed at an end, and the other courtesans were about to retrace their steps when another woman, a belated arrival, was seen upon the threshold. She had nothing in her hand, and it seemed as if she also had naught but her beauty to offer. Her hair appeared as two streams of gold, two deep waves full of shade, which engulfed the ears and were twisted in seven rolls over the back of the neck. The nose was delicate, with expressive nostrils which palpitated at times over a thick painted mouth, the corners rounded and throbbing. The flexible line of the body undulated at every step, animated by the rolling of the hips or the oscillation of the breasts, under which bent the supple waist.

Her eyes were extraordinary: blue but dark and bright at the same time, changing and glinting like moonstones, half closed under drooping lashes. Those eyes looked, as sirens sing . . .

The priest turned towards her, waiting for her to speak.

She said:

——

"Chrysis, O Chryseia, supplicates thee. Accept the poor gifts she lays at thy feet. Hear, love, and solace her that lives after thine example and for the cult of thy name, and grant her her prayers."

She held out her hands gilded with rings, and bent low with her legs close together.

The vague canticle began again. The murmur of the harps rose up towards the statue with the swirling fumes of crackling incense from the priest's censer.

"To thee, O Hetaira! . . . Chrysis consecrates her necklace."

She drew herself up slowly to her full height and offered a bronze mirror which hung from her girdle.

———

"To thee, Astarte of the Night, that joinest hand to hand and lip to lip, and whose symbol is like to the footprint of the deer upon the pale soil of Syria, Chrysis consecrates her mirror. It has seen the haggard darkness of the eyelids and the glitter of the eyes after love, the hair glued to the temples by the sweat of thy battles, O! warrior-queen of ruthless hand, thou that joinest body to body and mouth to mouth."

———

The priest laid the mirror at the feet of the statue. Chrysis drew from her golden hair a long comb of red copper, the planetary metal of the goddess.

"To thee," she said, "Anadyomene, born of the rosy dawn and the sea-foam's smile; to thee. O nudity shimmering with tremulous pearls, that didst bind thy dripping hair with ribbons of green seaweed, Chrysis consecrates her comb. It has plunged into her hair tossed by thy convulsions, O furiously-panting mistress of Adonis, that furrowest the camber of the loins and racks the stiffening knee!"

———

She gave the comb to the old man and inclined her head to the right in order to take off her emerald necklace.

———

"To thee", she said, "O! Hetaira, that drivest away the blushes of shamefaced maidens and promptest the lewd laugh, for whom we sell the love that streams from our entrails, Chrysis consecrates her necklace. It was given to her for her fee by a man whose name she knows not, and each emerald is a kiss on which thou hast lived an instant."

———

She made a last and more prolonged reverence, put the collar into the priest's hand and took a step as if to depart.

The priest stayed her:

"What do you ask of the goddess for these precious offerings?"

She shook her head, smiled, and said:

"I ask nothing."

Then she passed along the procession, stole a rose from a basket, and put it in her mouth as she went out.

One by one all the women followed. The door closed upon the empty temple.

———

Demetrios remained alone, concealed in the bronze pedestal.

He had not lost a gesture or a word of all this scene, and when everything was over, he remained motionless for a long time, harassed by new torments, passionate, irresolute.

He had thought himself quite cured of his madness of the night before, and had believed that henceforth nothing could throw him a second time into the ardent shadow of this strange woman.

But he had counted without her.

Women! O women! if you wish to be loved, show yourselves, return, present yourselves! The emotion he had felt on her entrance was so entire and overwhelming that it was out of the question to dream of struggling against it by a violent effort of the will. Demetrios was bound like a barbarian slave to a triumphal car. The idea of escape was an illusion. Without knowing it, and quite naturally, she had made him her captive.

He had seen her coming in the distance, for she wore the same yellow robe she had had on the quay. She walked with low, supple steps and with languid undulations of the hips. She had come straight to him, as if she had divined him behind the stone.

He realised from the first instant that he was ready once more to fall at her feet. When she drew the mirror of polished bronze from her girdle, she looked at herself in it for the last time before giving it to the priest, and the brilliancy of her eyes became stupefying. When, in order to take her copper comb, she laid her hand upon her hair and raised her bended arm, in conformity with the gesture of the Graces, the beautiful line of her body revealed itself under the tissue, and the sun illumined a tiny dew of brilliant sweat under her armpit. Finally, when, in order to lift up and unbuckle her necklace of heavy emeralds, she parted the pleated silk that veiled her double bosom down to the sweet shade-hidden place that admits of nothing more than a bouquet being slipped into it, Demetrios was seized with such a frenzied desire to put his lips upon it and tear off the whole dress that . . . But Chrysis began to speak.

She spoke, and every one of her words was torture to him. She seemed wantonly to insist and enlarge upon the prostitution of the vase of beauty that she was, white as the statue itself, and full of overflowing gold streaming down in a shower of hair. She told how her door was open to the lounging passer-by, how her body was delivered over to the contemplation of the unworthy, how the task of firing her cheeks with the flush of passion was committed to clumsy children. She spoke of the venal fatigue of her eyes, of her lips hired by the night, of her hair entrusted to brutal hands, of her divinity crucified.

Even the exceeding facility of her access was a charm in Demetrios's eyes, though he was resolved to use it solely for his own benefit and to close the door behind him. For it is profoundly true that a woman only reaches the utmost limit of her seductiveness when she gives occasion for jealousy.

And so, having given the goddess her green necklace in exchange for the one she hoped for. Chrysis returned to the town carrying a human will in her mouth, like the little stolen rose whose stalk she was nibbling.

Demetrios waited until he was left alone in the temple; then he issued forth from his retreat.

He looked at the statue apprehensively, expecting an infernal inward struggle. But, being incapable of renewing a violent emotion at so short an interval of time, he once more became astonishingly calm, without premature remorse.

Negligently, tranquilly, he climbed close up to the statue, took the necklace of true pearls from off Anadyomene's neck, and slipped it into his raiment.

VII
THE TALE OF THE ENCHANTED LYRE

He walked very rapidly, hoping to overtake Chrysis in the road which led to the town. He was afraid that if he delayed any further he might once again lose his courage and his power of will.

The white, hot road was so luminous that Demetrios closed his eyes as if the midday sun was shining. He was walking in this way without looking in front of him, when he narrowly escaped colliding with four black slaves who were marching at the head of a fresh procession. Suddenly a musical little voice said softly:

"Well-beloved, how glad I am!"

He raised his head: it was Queen Berenice leaning on her elbow in her litter.

She gave the order:

"Stop, porters!"

And held out her arms to her lover.

Demetrios was greatly put out, but he could not refuse, and he got in sulkily.

Then Queen Berenice, beside herself with joy, crawled on her hands and knees to the far end, and rolled in the cushions like a playful kitten.

For this litter was a chamber carried by four and twenty slaves. It afforded ample room for twelve women to recline in it at random, upon a thick blue carpet strewn with stuffs and cushions; and its height was so great that one could not touch the roof, even with the tip of one's fan. Its length was greater than its width, and it was closed in front and on the three sides by very fine yellow curtains which scintillated with light. The back was of cedar-wood, draped in a long veil of orange-coloured silk. At the top of this splendid wall, the great golden hawk of Egypt hung grimly with its two wings extended to their full extent. Lower down, carved in ivory and silver, the antique symbol of Astarte gaped above a lighted lamp whose rays strove with the daylight in elusive reflections. Underneath, lay Queen Berenice, fanned on either side by two Persian slave women, waving two tufts of peacock's feathers.

She beckoned the young sculptor to her side with her eyes, and repeated:

"Well-beloved, I am happy!" She stroked his cheek.

"I was looking for you, Well-beloved. Where were you? I have not seen you since the day before yesterday. If I had not met you I should soon have died of grief. I was so unhappy all alone in this great litter. I have thrown all my jewels over the bridge of Hermes, to make circles in the water. You see I have neither rings nor necklace. I look like a little pauper at your feet."

She turned round to him and kissed him on the mouth.

The two fan-bearers sat down upon their haunches a little further off, and when Queen Berenice began to speak in a low tone, they put their fingers close to their ears in order to make a semblance of not hearing. But Demetrios did not answer, barely listened, remained like one bewildered. He saw of the young queen nothing but the red smile of her mouth and the black cushion of her hair which she always wore loosely bound in order to be able to rest her weary head upon it.

But Demetrios did not answer.

She said:

"Well-beloved, I have wept during the night. My bed was cold. When I awoke, I stretched my naked arms to my two sides and I did not find you, and my hand nowhere met the hand I embrace to-day. I waited for you in the morning, and you had not been since the full moon. I sent slaves into all the quarters of the town and I had them executed when they came back without you. Where were you? were you at the temple? you were not in the garden with those strange women? No, I see by your eyes that you have not loved. Then what were you doing far away from me? You were before the statue? Yes, I am sure you were there. You love it more than me now. It is exactly like me, it has my eyes, my mouth, my breasts, but it is the statue that

- 64 -

you treasure. I am a poor deserted woman. I weary you, and I see it well. You think of your marble and your ugly statues as if I were not more beautiful than all of them, and, in addition, alive, amorous, and tender, ready to grant you whatever you are willing to accept, resigned whenever you refuse. But you want nothing. You have refused to be a king, you have refused to be a god and be adored in a temple of your own. You almost refuse to love me now."

She gathered her feet under her and leaned upon her hand.

"I would do anything to see you at the palace, Well-beloved. If you do not want me any longer, tell me who it is that attracts you, she shall be my friend. The . . . the women of my court . . . are beautiful. I have a dozen also who have been kept in ignorance of the very existence of men. They shall all be your mistresses if you will come to see me after them. . . And I have others with me who have had more lovers than the sacred courtesans and are expert in love. Choose which you will, I have also a thousand foreign slave-women; you shall have any of them you please. I will dress them like myself, in yellow silk and silver.

"But no, you are the most beautiful and the coldest of men. You love no one, you suffer yourself to be loved, you lend yourself, out of charity, to those who are captured by your eyes. You permit me to have my pleasure of you, but as an animal allows itself to be milked, looking somewhere else all the time. Ah! Gods! Ah! Gods! I shall end by being able to do without you, young coxcomb that the whole town adores, and from whom no woman can draw tears. I have other than women at the palace; I have sturdy Ethiopians with chests of bronze and arms bulging out with muscles. In their embrace, I shall soon forget your womanish legs and your pretty beard. The spectacle of their passion will doubtless be a new one for me, and I shall give my amorousness a rest. But the day I am certain that your eyes have ceased to trouble me by their absence, and that I can replace your mouth, then I shall despatch you from the top of the bridge of Hermes to join my necklace and my rings like a jewel I have worn too long. Ah! what it is to be a queen!"

She sat up and seemed as if waiting. But Demetrios remained impassive, and did not move a muscle, as if he had not heard her. She resumed angrily:

"You have not understood?"

He leaned carelessly upon his elbow and said quietly and unmovedly:

"I have thought of a tale.

———

"Long ago, long before the conquest of Thrace by your father's ancestors, it was inhabited by wild beasts and a few timorous men.

"The animals were very beautiful: there were lions tawny as the sun, tigers striped like the evening, and bears black as night.

"The men were little and flat-nosed, covered with old, worn skins, armed with rude lances and bows without beauty. They shut themselves up in mountain holes, behind huge stones which they moved with difficulty. They passed their lives at the chase. There was blood in the forests.

"The country was so forlorn that the gods had deserted it. When Artemis left Olympus in the whiteness of the morning, she never took the path which would have led her to the North. The wars which were waged there did not disturb Ares. The absence of pipes and flutes repelled Apollo. The triple Hecate alone shone in solitude, like the face of a Medusa upon a petrified land.

"Now, there came to live in that country a man of more favoured race, one who did not dress in skin like the mountain savages.

"He wore a long white robe which trailed behind him a little. He loved to wander at night in the calm forest-glades by the light of the moon, holding in his hand a little tortoise-shell in which were fixed two auroch-horns. Between these horns were stretched three silver strings.

"When his fingers touched the strings, delicious music passed over them, much sweeter than the sound of fountains, or the murmur of the wind in the trees, or the swaying of the barley. The first time he played, three sleepy tigers awoke, so prodigiously charmed that they did him no harm, but approached as near as they could and retired when he ceased. On the morrow there were many more, and wolves also, and hyenas, and snakes poised upright on their tails.

"After a very short time the animals came of their own accord, and begged him to play to them. A bear would often come quite alone to him and go away enchanted on hearing three marvellous chords. In return for his favours, the wild beasts provided him with food and protected him against the men.

"But he tired of this tedious life. He became so certain of his genius, and of the pleasure he afforded to the beasts, that he ceased to care to play well. The animals were always satisfied, so long as it was he who played. Soon he refused even to give them this satisfaction, and stopped playing altogether, from indifference. The whole forest mourned, but for all that the musician's threshold did not lack savoury meats and fruits. They continued to nourish him, and loved him all the more. The hearts of beasts are so constructed.

"Now one day, he was leaning against his open door, looking at the sunset behind the motionless trees, when a lioness happened to pass by. He took a step inside as if he feared tiresome solicitations. The lioness did not trouble about him, and simply passed by.

"Then he asked her in astonishment; 'Why do you not beg me to play?' She answered that she cared nothing about it. He said to her: 'Do you not know me?' She answered: 'You are Orpheus.' He answered: 'And you don't want to hear Me?' She repeated, 'No.' 'Oh!' he cried, 'oh! how I am to be pitied! It is just for you that I should have liked to play. You are much more beautiful than the others, and you must understand so much better. If you will listen to me one little hour, I will give you everything you can dream of.' She answered: 'Steal the fresh meats that belong to the men of the plain. Assassinate the first person you meet. Take the victims they have offered to your gods, and lay all at my feet.' He thanked her for the moderation of her demands, and did what she required.

"For one hour he played before her: but afterwards he broke his lyre and lived as if he were dead."

The queen sighed:

"I never understand allegories. Explain it to me, Well-beloved. What does it mean?"

He rose.

"I do not tell you this in order that you may understand. I have told you a tale to calm you a little. It is late. Good-bye, Berenice."

She began to weep.

"I was sure of it! I was sure of it!"

He laid her like a child upon her soft bed of luxurious stuffs, imprinted a smiling kiss upon her unhappy eyes, and tranquilly descended from the great litter without stopping it.

CPSIA information can be obtained
at www.ICGtesting.com
Printed in the USA
LVHW052357021121
702257LV00007B/830

9 789355 349842